The Magic Christmas Kite

Marilynn J. Harris

Cottage Publishing

Cottage Publishing
Boise, Idaho
www.marilynnjharris.com

©2015 Marilynn J. Harris. All rights reserved

No part of this book may be reproduced, stored in a retrieval system, or transmitted by any means without the written permission of the author.

First published by Cottage Publishing – October 19, 2015

ISBN-13: 978-1517708627 (CreateSpace)

ISBN-10: 1517708621

Printed in the United States of America

For information or to order more books please visit our website:
www.marilynnjharris.com

Or Contact:
**Cottage Publishing
8530 W Targee Street
Boise, ID 83709**

The Family

To my Legacy

My seven grandchildren

Jeffrey Michael
Darrek Lee
Hailie Nicole
Devon Levi
Kennedy Raine
Greyson James
Emerson Claire

Luke 2: 11 KJV
For unto you is born this day in the city of David
a Savior, which is Christ the Lord.

I had a magic Christmas kite
My grandma gave to me
She said that it would come to life
When placed beneath the tree

She told me if I closed my eyes
And said a certain word
The kite would become magical
And travel like a bird

The kite was bright and colorful
But it didn't seem brand new
Still I found it quite amazing
And my cousins all did too

At first I said this couldn't be
But Grandma never lies
So I gathered all the cousins round
And we each closed our eyes

We sat around the Christmas tree
With all the lights aglow
And something started happening
But what, we didn't know

The kite started growing
And the room began to spin
Every object started floating
Soon the voyage would begin

My name is Jeffrey Michael
I'm the oldest of the group
With six younger cousins
I help organize our troop

Even though I am much older
On the night our flight began
We all became the same size
The same age; we all were ten

Darrek is the next in line
And he turned ten years too
Then Greyson, Devon, Kennedy
Baby Emerson, Hailie Loo

The little ones grew bigger
The older ones were small
We all became just ten years old
A perfect age for all

I think the reason we were ten
At ten we still believed
In the enchantment of the season
And the joy that we received

Each cousin started screaming
When the kite began to fly
Then we suddenly grasped the magic
As the world below flew by

Every house, tree and snowman
Looked small as we gazed down
We held on tight and giggled
As we swiftly left our town

The kite was shaped just like a ship
That sailed the seven seas
In front it had a Christmas wreath
That jiggled in the breeze

The Christmas kite was speeding
To where we didn't know
We held on tight and smiled
And were thankful we could go

All seven cousins were best friends
We always had such fun
And the mystery on that Christmas Eve
United us as one

We flew across America
Our hearts were filled with glee
With no idea where we might stop
We had to wait and see

The Christmas kite was soaring fast
The stars were rushing by
But none of us were frightened
By the darkness of the sky

Suddenly the world around
Was filled with a bright glow
An angel came to spread the news
To the shepherds down below

We stared out in amazement
To see the blessed sight
The glory of the heavens shone
And lit up all the night

We watched the shepherds cower
As the angel spoke to them
About a new born baby
Who would save the world from sin

It seemed like only moments
Once again the kite took flight
To seek the tiny baby
Who brought peace to earth that night

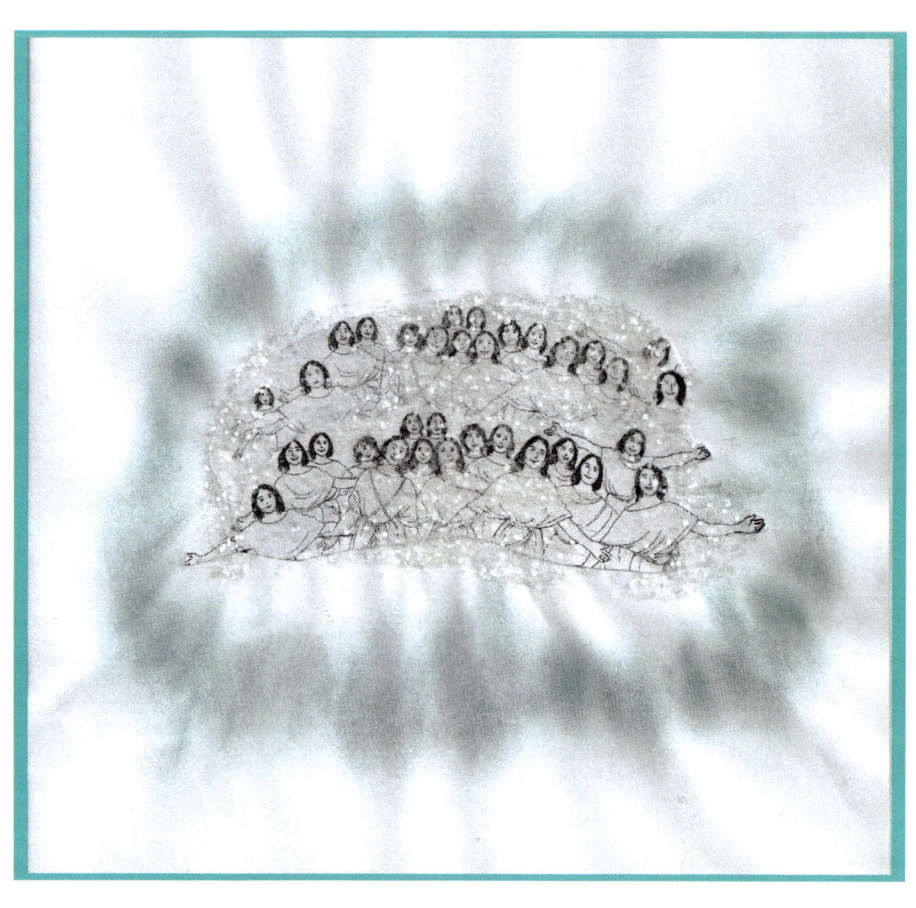

The angels were all singing
It was such a glorious sound
The heavens were so joyful
There were choirs all around

As we hovered over the manger
Where the Baby Jesus lay
We bowed our heads and thanked the Lord
All we could do was pray

We stared down at the infant
It was such a Holy sight
At ten years old we understood
The Christmas story was right

The child was wrapped in swaddling clothes
Just like the Bible said
And everyone around him
Knelt and bowed their heads

The Wise men brought him presents
The shepherds had their sheep
And we saw the love on Mary's face
As she watched the baby sleep

It was such a hallowed setting
And we were blessed that night
To live the Christmas story
As we gazed down from the kite

Our hearts would never be the same
We knew that it was true
The Son of God had come to earth
To save both me and you

Rapidly the magic kite
Began to shake and heave
We must go home and tell the world
We truly do believe

Suddenly in just a flash
We opened up our eyes
Our Grandma stood before us
And she didn't seemed surprised

She smiled the way that Grandmas do
And told us welcome back
She handed us some cookies
And hot chocolate for a snack

We quickly told her of our trip
All seven talked at once
But Grandma only listened
And smiled at us a bunch

When finally it was quiet
Our grandma told us all
That she had ridden in the kite
When she was very small

She too had seen the shepherds
And had heard the angels sing
She told us of the wise men
Who brought presents to the King

She also saw the Holy child
And that's why she believed
The magic kite would take us back
To that first Christmas Eve

Dec. 2015

To Railey
From Grandma Kathy &
Papa Kevin

ALWAYS BELIEVE

Blessings
Idaho Author
Marilyn J Harris
Boise New Hope

Made in the USA
Charleston, SC
29 October 2015